Zeke and His
Level A • Book 2

A Zoo-phonics® Reader

The Authors and Developers of The Zoo-phonics Language Arts Program
Georgene E. Bradshaw, Irene M. Clark and Charlene A. Wrighton

Illustrators
Irene M. Clark, Cynthia Clark and Matthew Anderson

Allie Alligator

 has lots and lots of pals.

Bubba **B**ear

 swims in a pond.

Catina Cat

 has a soft bed.

Deedee Deer

D can toss moss.

Ellie Elephant

 **E** stacks logs in the fog.

Francy Fish

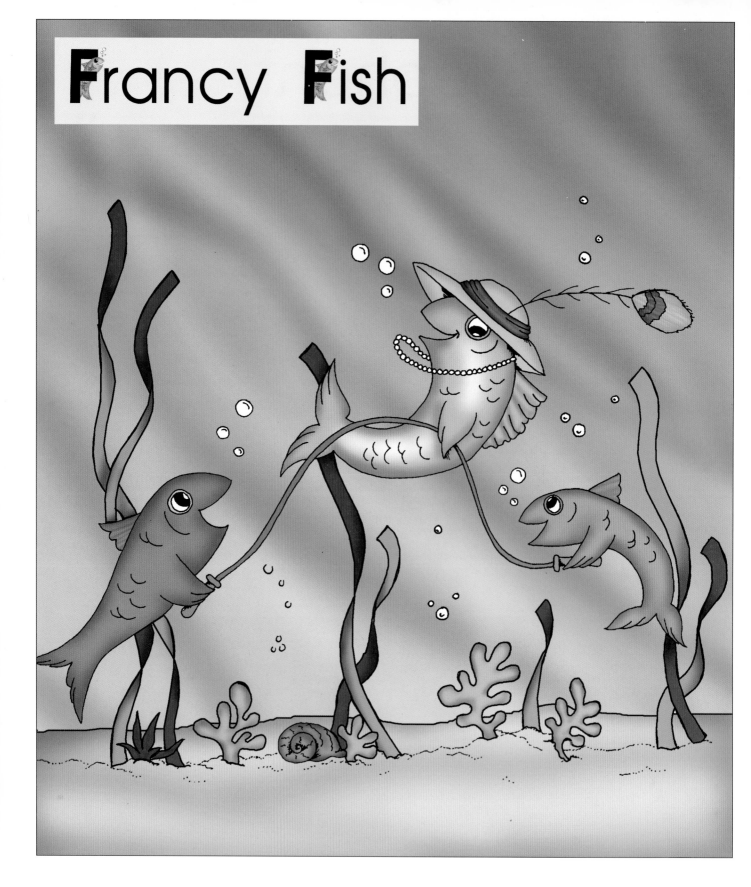

 flips and flops.

Gordo Gorilla

 has a grip and a grin.

Honey Horse

 trots fast.

Inny **I**nchworm

I drops on a twig.

Jerry Jellyfish

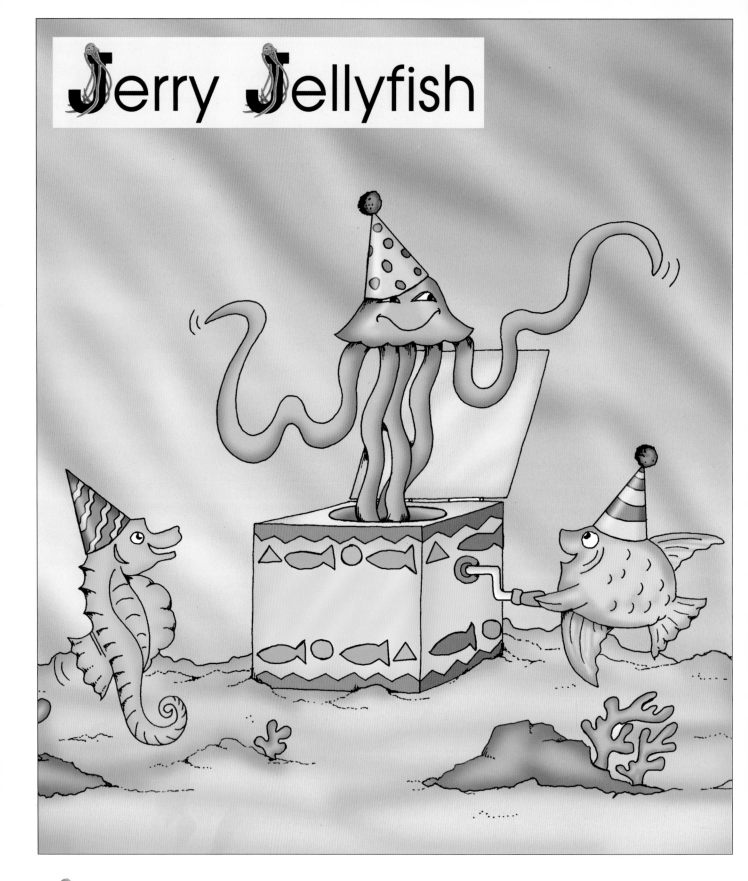

 is a Jack-in-the-Box.

Kayo Kangaroo

K can kick.

Lizzy Lizard

L lets bugs land.

Missy Mouse

 mends a mitt.

Nigel Nightowl

 will rap next.

Olive Octopus

 has lots of pots.

 spins a red top.

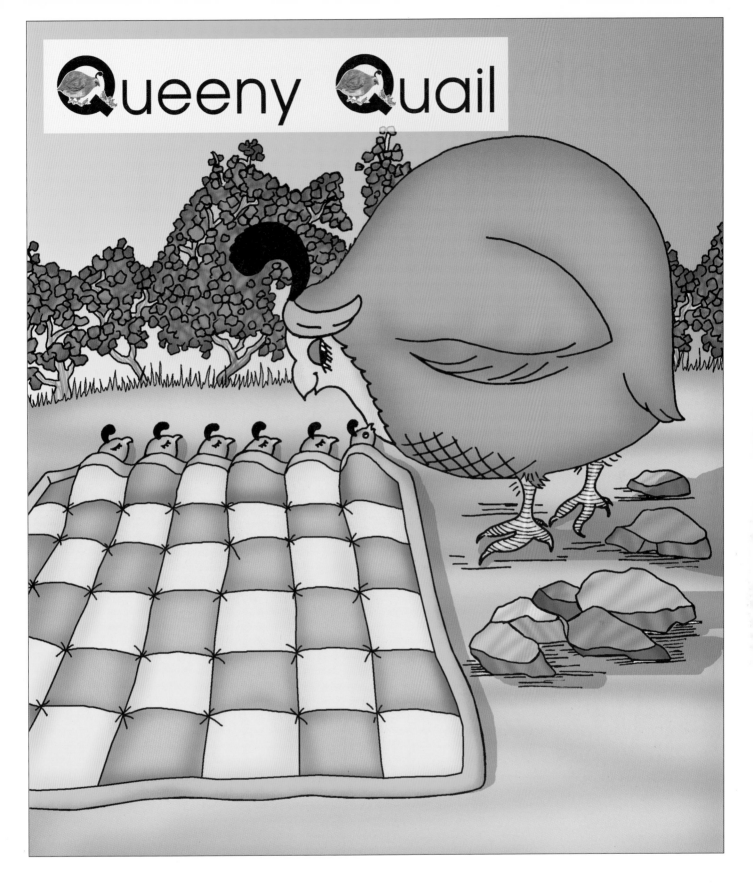

Queeny Quail

 has a quilt.

Robby Rabbit

 can hop and stop.

Sammy Snake

 slips and slips.

Timothy Tiger

 naps and still taps.

Umber Umbrella Bird

 can strum and hum.

Vincent **V**ampire Bat

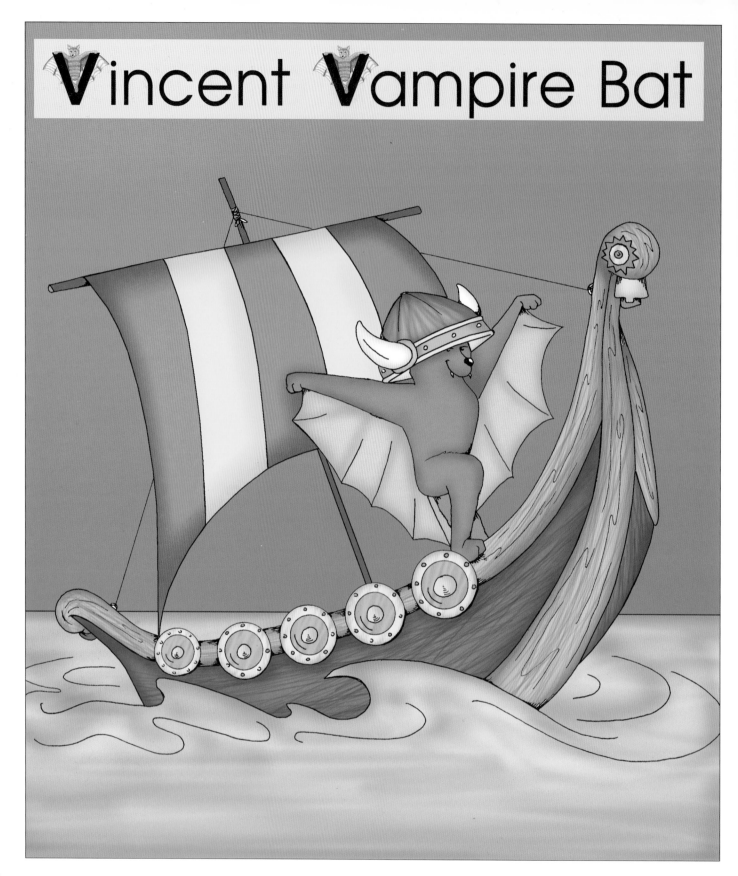

 has a hat.

Willie Weasel

 runs up a hill.

Xavier Fox

 bops at a sock hop.

Yancy Yak

 is on a trek.*

*To take a trip on foot, especially through a mountainous area, is called a trek.

Zeke Zebra

 has a job.

GUIDELINES FOR TEACHERS AND PARENTS

The *Zoo-phonics Reader® Level A Series* is designed to support the total Zoo-phonics Program of Phonics, Reading, Spelling and Writing.

Level A, Book 2, is geared to the child who has mastered the sounds and shapes of the alphabet, can spell out simple VC/CVC words, has completed Level A Book 1 and is ready to begin sound blending (regardless of age!). Remember that each child develops at his/her own pace, so not every child will be developmentally ready to read independently at this time. If they are not ready, simply give that child more time to develop an automaticity with the sounds and shapes of the alphabet. Play games such as "The Make It Say… Game" preparing him or her for word building and sound blending. (See the various manuals for more suggestions.)

As you work with individuals or groups, try these suggestions:

1. Use "Shadow Reading" (The Neurological Impress Method. See the internet for more information). This is the process:
    a. The Teacher/Parent reads the text aloud, first. Discuss any unfamiliar vocabulary.
    b. As you read the same text again, the child reads "under" the adult's voice. (The student attempts to read quietly at the same time as the adult.)
    c. The child then reads again with the adult, but this time the child's voice is stronger.
    d. The child then reads the text aloud, independently.

2. The child can trace the sentence with his/her finger while reading, allowing the finger to move ahead of the eye, actually pulling the eye in a left to right sequence. This "pulling" helps the eyes to move smoothly, enabling fluency in reading. In time, this will not be needed.

    The adult is to gently correct omissions, errors and substitutions "on the spot," asking the student to "Please Signal that word;" "Stop and try that again;" or say, "Let's Signal and sound that word together." In a classroom setting, you can ask the student who is reading to lead the class in sounds and Signals, thus building the student's confidence. *Each sound and Signal "event" is completed within half a minute's time or less.*

    Remember, it is the goal that students *master* new phonemes and vocabulary as they progress, thus the importance of Body Signals and sounds for placing new phonemic information into the brain for mastery, and retrieval. Students will very quickly **wean** themselves from having to give sounds and Signals for every grapheme or word. When they read words without Signaling or sounding, it means they now have the words in their memory. When they give sound and Signal they are in the process of memorizing the word, and cannot read it "on sight."

    > "…the awareness of phoneme segmentation does not develop spontaneously even by adulthood, but arises as a con-comitant of reading instruction and experience."[1]

3. Use the *Animal Alphabet Cards (Large or Small)* (located in the *Zoo-phonics® Kits*) for word building and sound blending, using the Word List, located in the back of this Reader.

4. Using the Word List try these two activities:

    a. The children take turns reading the words in the list. (Try to build speed.) If the child misses a word, the next child must begin at the top and read until s/he misses. The goal is to read the complete list without making an error. Remember that children can Sound and Signal the words for cueing and reinforcement, if needed. Have the child Signal, then read each word in the list quickly. (Signal, read word, Signal, read word, etc.)
    b. Have students take turns reading the words, using the words in sentences.

    Remember, getting through the word list is a team effort. If there is any sign of frustration from ANYONE, stop and go back to a prior reinforcement activity with the alphabet or word building and try again later.

    Remember, mastery is your goal and success your priority. Keep it light and keep it fun.

---

[1]The Alphabetic Principal and Learning to Read, by Isabelle Y. Liberman, Donald Shankweiler and Alvin M. Liberman. (Reprinted by the National Institute of Child Health and Human Development from Phonology and Reading Disability: Solving the Reading Puzzle.) - 1989

Word List
Reader Level A • Book 2
(in order of appearance in Reader)

*High Frequency Words

1. has*
2. lots
3. and*
4. of*
5. pals
6. swims
7. in*
8. a*
9. pond
10. soft
11. bed
12. can*
13. toss
14. moss
15. stacks
16. logs
17. the*
18. fog
19. flips
20. flops
21. grip
22. grin
23. trots
24. fast*
25. drops
26. on*
27. twig
28. is*
29. jack
30. box
31. kick
32. lets*
33. bugs
34. land
35. mends
36. mitt
37. will*
38. rap
39. next*
40. pots
41. spins
42. red*
43. top
44. quilt
45. hop
46. stop*
47. slips
48. naps
49. still*
50. taps
51. strum
52. hum
53. hat
54. runs*
55. up*
56. hill
57. bops
58. at*
59. sock
60. trek
61. job

Animal Names:

Allie Alligator

Bubba Bear

Catina Cat

Deedee Deer

Ellie Elephant

Francy Fish

Gordo Gorilla

Honey Horse

Inny Inchworm

Jerry Jellyfish

Kayo Kangaroo

Lizzy Lizard

Missy Mouse

Nigel Nightowl

Olive Octopus

Peewee Penguin

Queeny Quail

Robby Rabbit

Sammy Snake

Timothy Tiger

Umber
Umbrella Bird

Vincent
Vampire Bat

Willie Weasel

Xavier Fox

Yancy Yak

Zeke Zebra

Questions For Comprehension
Reader Level A • Book 2

Directions for Teacher/Parent: The first set of questions for each page relate directly from the text or the picture (Comprehensive Questions). The second set of questions (yellow box) require more information and a little more time (Teacher Directed Analysis). Often, the questions require students to conjecture and analyze from inference or prior knowledge. Where prior knowledge is needed, the teacher can share specific information so the children can then answer the questions. You can also ask other questions from the "Nature Notes" placed in both the *Zoo-phonics® Adventuresome Kids Manual* and the *Zoo-phonics® Nature Cards.* Note: Capital letters are used in text, now. Remember to have your students Signal out capital letters for extra reinforcement.

Teacher Directed Analysis.

CP = Children Pantomime

1. What does Allie Alligator "have lots of?" (She has lots of pals.)
2. Look at the picture. How many pals does Allie have? (six)
3. Which one is Allie Alligator? (the one with the bow) How do you know? (Because the children have seen Allie's picture many times. Prior knowledge)

1. Where do you think Allie lives? (In the swampy lowlands of the southern part of the United States. Show location on map)
2. What is the mood of Allie and her pals? (Answers may vary.)
3. What do you think the pals in the water might be saying? ("Come on in, the water is fine." Accept all answers.)

1. What is Bubba Bear doing? (He is swimming.)
2. Where is he swimming? (He is swimming in a pond.) What is a pond? (It is a very small body of water.)
3. Who is going along for the ride? (a bug)

1. As he swims, what stroke is Bubba using? (He uses the backstroke.) *CP*
2. What other bodies of water are there? (Streams, lakes, rivers, puddles, swamps, creeks, seas, ocean, brooks, etc.)

1. What does Catina Cat have? (a soft bed)
2. What time does the clock say? (3:35) Is it morning or night? (It is probably in the afternoon, because she is awake. Usually you sleep at 3:35 in the morning, but you never know. Maybe she couldn't sleep. This is called, "implied" information. You just have to guess.)

1. What can you tell about Catina? (She likes to read. She is comfortable by herself. She likes pretty things, etc.)
2. What is Catina Cat drinking? (It could be tea, coffee, hot milk, hot cocoa, etc.)
3. What kind of a story do you think she is reading? (Answers will vary.)

1. What can Deedee Deer do? (She can toss moss.)
2. Take a look at the picture. Why do you think she is tossing moss? (It looks like she is making a salad using the moss.) How do you know this? (She has a chef's hat on her head. Moss is in a bowl. There is salt and vinegar/oil on the table.) Do you think she will share the salad with someone? (Answers may vary.)

1. If you were lost in the woods, how could you tell in which direction to go? (Look for moss on the trees. Moss usually grows on the north side.) What should you do if you are lost? (Suggestions will vary: stay in one spot. Call for help. Ask someone "safe" for help. Do not go with anyone you do not know.)

2. Name other ways you can tell direction. (You can use a compass. The sun rises in the east and sets in the west. In olden days, and even today, people tell direction by the stars.)

1. What is Ellie Elephant doing? (She is stacking logs.)

2. Where is Ellie stacking logs? (in the fog)

3. What is that piece of paper on the tree for? (She is keeping track of the logs she has stacked.) Look at the tally marks. How many has she stacked? (8) How many tally marks are there? (8) After she stacks the one in her trunk, how many tally marks will there then be? (9) Teach the children how to tally.

4. What is funny about how Ellie is holding the pencil? (She is holding it with her tail.)

1. What kind of hat is Ellie wearing? (She is wearing a visor. It keeps the sun out of her eyes.)

2. If you had a tail, what things might you do with it? (Swing from tree to tree, hold a toothbrush, swat flies, dust cobwebs, etc.)

1. What is Francy Fish doing? (She is flipping and flopping.) Look at the picture. What is she really doing? (She is jumping rope with seaweed.)

2. Which one is Francy? (She is the one with the hat and pearls.) How do you know? (Answers will vary.)

1. What song might Francy and her friends be singing? ("I'm Forever Blowing Bubbles," or "The Jump Rope Rap" from the *Zoo-phonics Music That Teaches CD*.)

2. Raise your hand if you like to jump rope at recess. (Count the number of boys. Count the number of girls. Discuss the fact that many athletes jump rope to train their muscles.)

1. What does the sentence say that Gordo Gorilla has? ("A grip and a grin") Discuss both of these words. Ask children to demonstrate both. How many things is Gordo gripping? (2)

2. Look at the picture. What is Gordo doing? (He is holding a bunch of bananas while swinging from a vine.)

1. What is the opposite of a tight grip? (It is a loose grip.)

2. Who else swings from a vine? (Tarzan does.) Everyone give a Tarzan call.

3. From the picture, what do you know about Gordo? (He likes bananas. He is happy. He is a big animal. He lives in the jungle. He is clever, etc.)

1. What does the sentence say Honey Horse is doing? (She is trotting.)

2. How does she do it? (She trots fast.) Signal/Sound "fast," and then another word that means the same thing ("quick").

3. What and who is she pulling? (She pulls a cart and a little girl.) Does the girl look happy or scared? (She looks happy.) How do you know this? (The picture shows her smiling. Pictures can help us to understand the text.)

1. What things make Honey look dressed up? (Her hat has flowers and bows on it. The reins have flowers on them.)
2. Discuss the parts of the cart. (reins, seat, wheels, harness)
3. Who would like to ride in this cart? (Take a show of hands.) How many of you have ridden in a horse-drawn cart before? (Again, they raise their hands.)
4. Who would like to be Honey? Who would like to be the child?
5. What do you think the little girl is thinking? (The little girl may be thinking, "This is fun!" or "Faster, faster!" Honey might be thinking, "I sure deserve my oats today!" or "I can run as fast as the wind.")

1. What is Inny Inchworm doing? (He is dropping down on a twig.) What does the word, "drop" imply? (That he is coming from higher up.)
2. Discuss the word, "twig." (It is a small branch from a tree.) Can we tell from this where Inny lives? (He lives in oak trees. The picture shows this.)

1. Learn about moths and butterflies. Look at the *Zoo-phonics Nature Cards.* Is Inny really a worm? (He is a male larva which turns into a moth.) What does the female become? (She becomes a wingless beetle.)
2. Is Inny herbivorous (eats fruits and vegetables), carnivorous (eats meat), or omnivorous (eats both)? (Inny is herbivorous.) Discuss the meaning of each word and review them often.
3. Inny is "rappeling." What does this mean? (Inny lets himself down on a silken thread that comes from a gland near his mouth in liquid form and hardens in the air. See *Zoo-phonics Nature Cards*.) Can humans rappel? (Yes, mountain climbers and cave explorers rappel.)

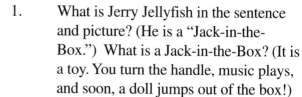

1. What is Jerry Jellyfish in the sentence and picture? (He is a "Jack-in-the-Box.") What is a Jack-in-the-Box? (It is a toy. You turn the handle, music plays, and soon, a doll jumps out of the box!)
2. Look at the picture. Describe what you see. (Answers will vary. The children should describe the sea creatures and their party hats.) Discuss why they might be wearing party hats. Do sea creatures really wear party hats? Is this fantasy or reality? (It is fantasy or make-believe.)
3. Everybody, pretend you are a jack-in-the-box. *CP*

1. Who are Jerry's friends? (a fish and a sea horse) Learn about sea horses.
2. What nursery rhyme is similar to a jack-in-the-box? (The nursery rhyme, "Jack be nimble, Jack be quick, Jack jump over the candlestick" is similar.)

1. What can Kayo Kangaroo do? (He can kick.) Stand up and kick like Kayo.
2. Everyone Signal the word, "kick." Do you see how Catina and Kayo work together to make the "k" sound?
3. The sentence says he "can" kick. Do you think he is very good at this? (The answers will vary.)

1. What is Kayo practicing? (He is practicing kicking a football.)
2. Everyone get into a huddle. Now, pantomime "hiking" the ball, kicking the ball, kicking in Tae Kwon Do, dancing, etc. (Let the children come up with other ideas.)

1. What does Lizzy Lizard let bugs do? (She lets them land.) Where? (on her head and back)
2. What does the picture remind you of? (an airstrip where planes land) Does Lizzy seem to mind bugs landing on her? (No.) How do you know? (She has a smile on her face.)

1. What is funny about this picture? (The bugs look like airplanes coming in for a landing.) Is this possible? (Yes, bugs do land on animals and people, but we most often brush them away.)
2. Do you know what that tall tree-like plant is called? (It is a saguaro cactus.) What is on top of it? (A windsock like you'd find at an airport is on top. It tells pilots which way the wind is blowing. The windsock helps pilots to take off and land their airplanes.)

1. What does Missy Mouse do? (She mends a mitt.) What is a "mitt?" (It is something you might put on your hand to protect it from the heat of the oven when cooking.) What does this word sound similar to? (Mittens, which also go on the hands to protect them from the cold.)
2. Look at Missy's face. Tell how she might be feeling. (Content, happy, etc.)

1. What is the difference between a mitt and a glove? (A mitt, or mitten, has a separate part for the thumb; gloves have separate parts for all four fingers and thumb.)
2. Study the wallpaper. Copy the pattern on paper, then from memory see whether you can draw Missy mending a mitt.

1. What does the sentence tell you? (That Nigel Nightowl will rap next) But, Nigel is holding the microphone. What does this tell you? (The other birds have already "rapped" and now it is his turn.) Is this stated or implied information? (It is implied, because you have to read the text, look at the picture, and then think.)
2. Look at the picture. Are they in the city or the country? (They are in the city. It looks like New York City, or somewhere similar.) What is the difference between the city and the country?

1. What does "rapping" mean to you? Allow the children to describe what they think "rap" is. (Spoken words, sometimes rhyming, with strong rhythmic beat and movement) Play the "Jump Rope Rap" from the *Zoophonics Music That Teaches* CD.
2. If you were a rapper, how would you dress? (Answers will vary.)
3. Take turns rapping and dancing.

1. What does Olive Octopus have in her "hands"? (She has lots of pots.)
2. What is Olive doing? (She is cooking.) What do you think she is stirring in the pot? (Pudding, soup, stew, etc.)
3. Discuss the fact that "oct" in octopus means "eight." Show an octogon. What about October? It is the tenth month. Why isn't it the eighth month? (It used to be the eighth month, but they added two more months to the calendar a long time ago. See explanation in Reader A, Book 1, page 34.)

1. What is the proper name for an octopus' arms? (Tentacles) What do they do? (They have suction cups that grab and hold onto prey.)

2. Draw a picture or act out what clean-up time for Olive might be like. (Pretend someone has lots of arms. Have one child stand in front while others stand behind him or her waving their arms. Make sure there are eight tentacles. How many children would that take? (Ask your students to figure this out. It would take four.)

1. What does the sentence tell you is happening? (It says that Peewee Penguin is spinning a red top.) Which word is the noun? (Top) Which is the verb? (Spins) Which is the adjective? (Red) Reinforce this often. Try other words with these parts of speech.
2. What else does the picture show? Have the children describe it in detail.

1. What is Peewee doing? (He is spinning a top.) What kind of act is Peewee doing? (He is doing a "balancing act.") Every-one stand and balance on one foot. Does it help to hold your arms out?
2. What kind of costume is Peewee wearing? (It is a costume from China.) Locate China on the globe or map.
3. Why is he holding parasols? (To help him balance.) What is another word for parasol? (umbrella) How does a parasol and an umbrella differ? (One is for the rain and one is for the sun.)

1. What does Queeny Quail have? (She has a quilt.)
2. What is a quilt? (It is a kind of blanket that keeps you warm.) Who is this blanket keeping warm? (Queeny's six babies.)
3. Tell how Queeny's babies might be feeling? (Sleepy, comfortable, warm, snuggly, rested, safe, happy)

1. What do Queeny and her babies have on the tops of their heads? (a crest of feathers on their head, sometimes called a "topknot." In other parts of the U. S. A., only the male quail has the feathers; however, both male and female California quail have feathers. The quail is the California State Bird.)
2. What other Zoo-phonics bird has a crest of feathers? (Umber Umbrella Bird)

1. What two things can Robby Rabbit do? (He can hop and stop.)
2. For what is he stopping? (There is a snail in the way of his jump. Or, maybe he is hopping over the snail and he has to stop at the stop sign. Maybe they are playing leaf-frog or "leap-snail." Ask children to guess.)
3. Signal the word, "stop." What does this important word mean? Where have you seen this word before? (On road signs) What color are the signs? (red)

1. Look at the faces of both Robby and the snail. What do you see? (They are both smiling, having a good time.) Does this look like a serious race or game? (Discuss.)
2. Play a game of "leap-snail." Have half the class be snails, and the other half be rabbits. Then, change roles.

S 1. What does Sammy Snake do? (He slips and slips.) What does this mean? (It means that he slithers along.) Move your hand like Sammy Snake as he "slips" through the sand or dirt.

2. Have the students describe the picture in detail. Who else is in the picture? (Another snake taking a nap.) Who do you think this snake is? (Maybe he is a relative of Sammy's or a friend.) What kind of hat is he wearing? (sombrero)

Activity: Hand out drawing paper and have the children sketch the scene, including as many objects and details as they can remember. Have them complete their sketches by adding color with colored pencils or crayons. Display the finished work on a bulletin board. Try this with other pages.

1. What does Timothy Tiger do? (He naps and still taps.) Why is he taking such a long nap? (He is having a wonderful dream that he is a tap dancer.)

2. Read the title of the book that Timothy has been reading. (<u>Hollywood Musicals</u>) Clap out "Hollywood." Clap out "Musicals." How many syllables are in each? (3)

1. What is the subject of Timothy's dream? (Answers may vary. However, you can see a picture of what Timothy is dreaming of in the bubble over his head. Most likely, he is dreaming that he is dancing in a Hollywood Musical.)

2. What is Timothy lying on? (It is a small bed or a couch. It has a fancy French word, "chaise lounge." It is pronounced "shaz-long.")

3. Does anyone know what this fancy lamp is made to look like? (A Tiffany lamp. Louis Comfort Tiffany, 1848 – 1933, was the creator of colored glass lampshades and vases, etc. They are very expensive. His artwork is still copied today.)

1. What can Umber Umbrella Bird do? (He can strum and hum.) What does this mean? (It means he can strum an instrument and hum a song at the same time.)

2. To whom is he strumming and humming? (There is a friend in the hut.) Who is this friend? (The children guess.) Is it male or female? (It is a female. She has no topknot or umbrella.)

3. Look at the picture. Where do you think Umber is? (He looks like he is in Hawaii or somewhere tropical.)

1. Where do Umbrella Birds live? (Have the children guess. Show them Central America and Northern South America on the map.)

2. What do you see that looks Hawaiian? (Answers will vary. Umber is wearing a hawaiian shirt and a lei; he is on a beach near a grass shack and palm trees; he is strumming a musical instrument called a ukulele.) Discuss these words.

Activity: Have the children plan and participate in a mini-luau.

a. The day before or the day of the luau, have the children make leis of paper flowers (crepe paper cut into small circles stretched, twisted and strung on thread) or leaves, etc.

b. Teach the children a few Hawaiian words: *wiki-wiki* = hurry; *hukilau* = a fishing party using nets; *lei* = a necklace made of flowers; *aloha* = "I love you," "hello," "good-bye;" *poi* = an Hawaiian food made from the taro root, cooked, pounded and eaten with two fingers.

c. Put on Hawaiian music and have the children improvise a hula dance.

d. For the feast, serve a fruit cup that might have pineapple, bananas, coconut, oranges and papayas. Serve vanilla yogurt instead of poi. Have them eat it with their two fingers, just like the Polynesian people did a long time ago.

1. What does Vincent Vampire Bat have on his head? (A funny looking hat.) Describe the hat. (The hat is round, has two horns, and is large. It might be made out of metal, animal horns, and leather.) It also might be called a helmet. Discuss this in terms of sports (football, bike, motorcycle riding, skate boarding, sports car racing, etc.)

2. Look at the picture. Describe Vincent and the boat in detail.

1. Who is Vincent dressed to look like? (Allow children to guess. He looks like a Viking. The Vikings were people from Scandinavia who were great seamen. They traveled in ships and conquered people from other countries.)

2. Look on the globe or map and locate these countries that make up Scandinavia (Norway, Sweden, Denmark, Finland, and Iceland).

3. Look at Vincent's ship. What kind is it? (It is a sailing ship with oars to help it move if there is no wind. It looks like a Viking ship.)

1. What does the sentence say Willie Weasel is doing? (He is running up a hill.) When you look at the picture, how can you tell he is running up hill? (The hill in the picture is drawn on a slant. The truck is tilted and Willie is leaning forward.)

2. Everyone stand and show how Willie looks running uphill. (The children pantomime.)

1. Who is driving the ice-cream truck? (Answers will vary. It might be his friend, his dad, cousin or uncle.) Could it even be a lady ice-cream truck driver? (The children discuss this idea.)

2. Do you think Willie is in good shape? (The children guess.) Does the picture or sentence give you this information? (No. We just have to look, read, think and then guess.)

3. Do you think he and the ice cream truck will make it up this hill? It is grassy and rocky. Is it really a road? (Answers will vary.)

1. What is Xavier Fox doing? (He is "bopping" at a sock hop.) Discuss the term, "sock hop." (It is a school dance that was especially popular during the 1940's and 1950's. The students wore saddle shoes and they would often end up dancing in their socks in the gymnasium to protect the wood floors.)

2. Look at the picture. Describe how the two are dressed. (Poodle skirt, vest, hat, socks, bow tie, ribbon, saddle shoes) Tell about the poodle skirts and saddle shoe fad.

1. On what kind of machine is Xavier's friend sitting? (It is called a jukebox. It is a coin-operated phonograph with push buttons to select the records. They still have them today, but most have CD's now.)
2. Can you think of another word that has "phon" in it? (The children guess: tele<u>phon</u>e, <u>phon</u>ograph, Zoo-<u>phon</u>ics.) What does this root word mean? (It means sound, voice and speech. It comes from the Latin, Greek and French languages.)

1. What is Yancy Yak doing? (He is on a "trek". He is hiking, walking and traveling.) Have the children describe the picture in detail.
2. What does the word "trek" mean? (It means to take a trip on foot, especially through a mountainous area.)
3. Look at the picture. Who is waving to him? (The children guess: His mom and dad, brothers, sisters, friends.) Is it stated information? (No. You must guess. We don't know even if this is Yancy's home. He could be visiting friends.)

1. Where has Yancy been? (Maybe to Mount Everest. It is a very tall mountain in the Central Himalayan Mountains on the border of Tibet and Nepal. Mt. Everest is 29,035 feet in height.) Now, how do we know he has climbed Mt. Everest? (We don't. We can only guess or pretend, because Yancy Yak is from this area.)

2. What kind of weather will Yancy find on Mt. Everest? (Have children guess. As one gets to the top, it is very cold, icy, snowy and windy. The oxygen is rare, so it is hard to breathe.)
3. What is Yancy wearing and carrying? (The children will identify the objects: a backpack, a rope, a sleeping bag, a fleece-lined cap with earflaps, to keep his ears warm, and high-top hiking boots.)

1. What does the picture tell you about Zeke Zebra? (Zeke has a job.) Look at the text in the picture. What does it say? Let's read it together: "Welcome to the Zoo." Where does Zeke work? (He works at the zoo.) Is this implied or stated information? (It is implied.)
2. What is Zeke doing? (He is selling cotton candy. Yum!)
3. Who is his customer? (Nigel Nightowl.)

1. Why do you think Nigel Nightowl is wearing a baseball cap? (To protect his eyes.) What is interesting about this? (Nigel only comes out at night, so his eyes aren't use to the daylight. This cap might protect his eyes.)
2. Where does Zeke keep his money? (Maybe he keeps it in his apron pocket or in the box on the cart.) Does the sentence or picture tell you this? (No. You have to think, then guess.)

"A Trip To The Zoo" — Classroom And Field Trip Activities • Books 1, 2 & 3

Since Zoo-phonics uses Animal Characters to teach children to read, spell and write, it is fitting that they learn specific facts about each Zoo-phonics Animal, as well as develop an appreciation of the animal kingdom in general.

PREPARATION FOR THE ZOO

As you plan for your trip to the zoo, use the following resources to prepare the children:

1. Find out what the children already know about the Animals and write the information on a flipchart.

2. Refer to the *Zoo-phonics Nature Cards* for further study.

3. Visit the school library and choose some books and magazines to bring back to your classroom to share. Make sure that they are fun or factual and have lots of pictures.

4. Use a globe or large map to discover where the Animals originate (Umbrella Bird…Central and South America; Yak…Tibet; Zebra…Africa, and so forth.)

5. On a flipchart, display a picture of a Zoo-phonics Animal. Write the description of each Animal as the children dictate. Ask the following questions to encourage their response:

    a. What does it look like? (tall, sleek, funny, soft, scary, etc.)
    b. What color is it? (tan, green, blue, etc.)
    c. What is the pattern of the fur or feathers? (striped, checked, wrinkled, etc.)
    d. What is the distinguishing feature? (tail, trunk, claws, topknot, etc.)
    e. How does it move? (flies, swims, jumps, hops, etc.)

    Encourage the children to use these descriptive and scientific words in their speaking and writing vocabulary.

6. Take time to talk about endangered species and which Zoo-phonics Animals are, or have been, on the Endangered Species List. (*Zoo-phonics Nature Notes* and *Saving Our Animal Friends*, September 1991, Vol. 7 and Vol. 12)

AT THE ZOO

1. Hand each child a reduced *Zoo-phonics Animal Alphabet Grid* checklist. Include the names of both school and child on the top of the page.

2. As the children come to a Zoo-phonics Animal, they are to check it off on the checklist (Grid). Of course, not all of the Zoo-phonics Animals will be found at every zoo.

3. Explain that during the zoo visit, time will be allowed to sketch and/or write about a favorite animal or scene. Provide each child with a small notebook and pencil. Don't forget your camera!

Allow the children the joy of discovery!